PRAYING
FOR AN ELECTION
A NON-PARTISAN, SCRIPTURE-BASED, PRAYER GUIDE

DAVID BUTTS

PrayerShop
Publishing

TERRE HAUTE, INDIANA

PrayerShop Publishing is the publishing arm of the Church Prayer Leaders Network. The Church Prayer Leaders Network exists to equip and inspire local churches and their prayer leaders in their desire to disciple their people in prayer and to become a "house of prayer for all nations." Its online store, prayershop.org, has more than 150 prayer resources available for purchase.

ISBN: 978-1-935012-91-7
E-Book ISBN: 978-1-935012-92-4

1 2 3 4 5 | 2024 2023 2022 2021 2020

THE POWER OF PRAYING FOR ELECTIONS

★ ★ ★ ★ ★

As intercessors, we have the God-given ability to change the history of our nation through fervent prayer and action. This holds especially true for elections! Praying for an Election is designed to provide Scripture-based prayer points and encourage you to journal your own God-directed prayers for the election process.

We are mobilizing the IFA army of intercessors to pray strategically for the Body of Christ to be salt and light in the civil arena. This is not a vague, general call to prayer. We have identified, through the wonders of technology, those who hold conservative values, are potentially fellow believers, and are not likely to vote. This silent majority, representing as many as 75% of the Church, could sway any election and every issue, if we are unified and active politically. You can pray for these potential voters at VoteYourValues2020.com–it makes a great complement to this prayer guide.

Use this guide throughout the election season, and the prayer resources and helps at IFApray.org. You will find over 100 prayer guides, special reports, and devotional series, as well as a library of great teaching videos, previous prayer calls and webcasts, and recorded prayers. Join the growing community of intercessors praying through key events at HeadlinePrayer.com.

From praying through this book, to praying for the potential voters at VoteYourValues.com, to prayer walking your town, to volunteering to monitor an election, to contacting your elected officials about election integrity, IFA wants to empower you as an intercessor to take action that complements your prayer. As we pray, and act, we will see God's purposes fulfilled in our nation!

PRAYING FOR AN ELECTION

Is positive change truly possible in our nation today?

In every election cycle, American Christians have amazing opportunities sandwiched between grave dangers. We are privileged to be a part of a nation of people who have the responsibility to choose their own leaders. For those believing that godly leaders are a source of blessing to a nation, elections provide us with great opportunity. However, when we begin to put our hope in leaders rather than in the Lord, we open ourselves to serious peril.

God's Word is very clear about having an undivided heart, trusting only in the Lord. King David, the mighty warrior, says, "Some trust in chariots and some in horses, but we trust in the name of the Lord our God" (Ps. 20:7). Awareness of this verse can create a tension in the thinking Christian. Some have overreacted and rejected the political process completely. Such people will be less motivated to pray over the elections.

A balanced and biblical approach, however, allows us to fully participate in the electoral process without falling into improperly placed trust.

In Paul's teaching on prayer in 1 Timothy 2:1–4, one of the major thrusts is praying for those in authority. According to Paul's reasoning, we want good government that allows us to live "peaceful and quiet lives"—ultimately freeing us to evangelize those who are lost.

Paul would have been amazed that Christians could someday actually take part in selecting those leaders. I believe he would have been even more amazed (and appalled) that many of those Christians didn't even bother to get involved in selecting their leaders for the purposes of God to be fulfilled.

Praying for the electoral process is the first step in seeing the fulfillment of what Paul is writing about to Timothy. I don't believe we should wait for a leader to be selected before we move into obedient prayer for those in authority. In prayer, we invite the Lord into the process of electing those leaders who will ultimately allow us to lead "peaceful and quiet lives in all godliness and holiness" (v. 2).

So why pray for the elections? There are a number of compelling reasons:

- The Bible commands us to pray for those who are in leadership, which would include those who are vying to become leaders.

- Godly leaders can help slow the erosion of religious liberties in our land, providing an increased window of opportunity for the Church to pray and evangelize.

- The selection of leaders who understand and lead according to God's righteous standards can bring great blessing to a nation (Prov. 14:34).

- Scripture also says, "For lack of guidance a nation falls, but many advisors make victory sure" (Prov. 11:14). The determination of who leads our nation will also determine who advises that leader and how we are guided.

PRAYING FOR OUR NATION, THE ELECTIONS, AND THE CHURCH

The following prayer points cover seven major areas that relate to our national elections, as well as some current flashpoints.

Note that there are more prayer points regarding the Church than any other area. As the Church goes, so goes the nation. Judgment most certainly begins in the house of God (1 Pet. 4:17).

This prayer guide is loosely structured for multiple uses. Choose from the suggested topics according to your interest and the leading of the Spirit. An individual might pick out a few prayer points from each category and pray those daily. A group might choose to divide them all among its members and cover the entire guide at one gathering. Some families or individuals may want to pray from this guide for months leading up to the election—and perhaps even beyond. Allow the Lord to lead you as you pray.

1. OUR NATION AND THE ISSUES IT FACES

★　★　★　★　★

Pray for the judges of this nation, that they will seek the wisdom that comes from above.

"But the wisdom that comes from heaven is first of all pure; then peace-loving, considerate, submissive, full of mercy and good fruit, impartial and sincere" (James 3:17).

Ask the Lord to thwart the efforts of those who would remove religious freedom from our nation.

"It is for freedom that Christ has set us free. Stand firm, then, and do not let yourselves be burdened again by a yoke of slavery" (Gal. 5:1).

Pray for truth to become valued again in American society.

"Then you will know the truth, and the truth will set you free" (John 8:32).

Pray that our nation will increasingly see that God is our only refuge in the midst of the troubles of this world.

"God is our refuge and strength, an ever-present help in trouble" (Ps. 46:1).

Pray for our judicial system and lawmakers—that justice for all, tempered by mercy and compassion, will guide our nation.

"God is our refuge and strength, an ever-present help in trouble" (Isa. 1:17). "This is what the Lord Almighty said: 'Administer true justice; show mercy and compassion to one another'" (Zech. 7:9).

Repent on behalf of our nation, because we have turned from making Scripture the basis of law, leaving behind wisdom and looking to ourselves for truth.

"We all, like sheep, have gone astray, each of us has turned to our own way; and the Lord has laid on him the iniquity of us all" (Isa. 53:6). "Then the Lord said to me, 'The prophets are prophesying lies in my name. I have not sent them or appointed them or spoken to them. They are prophesying to you false visions, divinations, idolatries and the delusions of their own minds'" (Jer.14:14).

Ask the Lord to pour out a spirit of repentance on our nation, that we might become a nation committed to following His ways.

"You will seek me and find me when you seek me with all your heart" (Jer. 29:13).

Pray that the U.S. will repent of its corporate rejection of the Word of God as the basis of law.

> *"How long will you who are simple love your simple ways? How long will mockers delight in mockery and fools hate knowledge? Repent at my rebuke! Then I will pour out my thoughts to you, I will make known to you my teachings" (Prov. 1:22–23).*

Pray that a holy fear of God will sweep across our nation, leading us back to a place of wisdom and walking in the LORD.

> *"Who among you fears the Lord and obeys the word of his servant? Let the one who walks in the dark, who has no light, trust in the name of the LORD and rely on their God" (Isa. 50:10).*

Scriptures and Personal Notes to Pray for Our Nation and Its Issues

2. THE ELECTION PROCESS

Pray for wisdom for voters and a safe and fair election.

"My son, do not let wisdom and understanding out of your sight, preserve sound judgment and discretion; they will be life for you, an ornament to grace your neck. Then you will go on your way in safety, and your foot will not stumble" (Prov. 3:21–23).

Ask the Lord to remove those who might try to unjustly and illegally change the outcome of the voting.

"I will make justice the measuring line and righteousness the plumb line; hail will sweep away your refuge, the lie, and water will overflow your hiding place" (Isa. 28:17).

Pray for a huge turnout of voters who use wisdom in their decisions.

"Get wisdom, get understanding; do not forget my words or turn away from them. Do not forsake wisdom, and she will protect you; love her, and she will watch over you" (Prov. 4:5–6).

Pray for protection from any attacks from enemies that would prevent or delay the election.

"Do not be afraid of them; the LORD your God himself will fight for you" (Deut. 3:22).

Scriptures and Personal Notes to Pray for the Election Process

3. CANDIDATES AND LEADERS

★　★　★　★　★

Pray for the salvation of those who are in leadership of our nation. Ask the Lord to remove all envy and selfish ambition.

"For where you have envy and selfish ambition, there you find disorder and every evil practice" (James 3:16).

Pray that candidates will take brave stands for righteousness, even when it may not be well received.

"Therefore put on the full armor of God, so that when the day of evil comes, you may be able to stand your ground, and after you have done everything, to stand. Stand firm then, with the belt of truth buckled around your waist, with the breastplate of righteousness in place" (Eph. 6:13–14). "If you do not stand firm in your faith, you will not stand at all" (Isa. 7:9b).

Pray that their families will be protected from harm and unnecessary scrutiny.

"You, LORD, will keep the needy safe and will protect us forever from the wicked, who freely strut about when what is vile is honored by the human race" (Ps. 12:7–8).

Ask the Lord to surround them with godly advisors.

"The fear of the LORD is the beginning of wisdom; all who follow his precepts have good understanding. To him belongs eternal praise" (Ps. 111:10).

Pray that each candidate will focus on the issues we face as a nation— and not on personal attacks on other candidates.

"If you bite and devour each other, watch out or you will be destroyed by each other" (Gal. 5:15).

Scriptures and Personal Notes to Pray for Candidates and Leaders

4. THE CHURCH

Pray for a spirit of humility in the Church and an outreach toward those whom the Bible calls the least among us.

"In the same way, you who are younger, submit yourselves to your elders. All of you, clothe yourselves with humility toward one another, because, 'God opposes the proud but shows favor to the humble'" (1 Pet. 5:5). "But God will never forget the needy; the hope of the afflicted will never perish" (Ps. 9:18). "The King will reply, 'Truly I tell you, whatever you did for one of the least of these brothers and sisters of mine, you did for me'" (Matt. 25:40).

Pray that the churches in your community and area will preach the gospel of Christ powerfully.

"For I am not ashamed of the gospel, because it is the power of God that brings salvation to everyone who believes: first to the Jew, then to the Gentile" (Rom. 1:16).

Thank the Lord for the freedom we have in Him and for the wisdom to understand that freedom.

"You, my brothers and sisters, were called to be free. But do not use your freedom to indulge the flesh; rather, serve one another humbly in love" (Gal. 5:13).

Pray for a spirit of consecration and holiness to come upon the Church in America.

"Joshua told the people, 'Consecrate yourselves, for tomorrow the Lord will do amazing things among you'" (Josh. 3:5). "But just as he who called you is holy, so be holy in all you do" (1 Pet. 1:15).

Pray for a spirit of compassion to come over the Church in this nation so that we will begin seriously to live out the lifestyle of Jesus in our communities.

"Therefore if you have any encouragement from being united with Christ, if any comfort from his love, if any common sharing in the Spirit, if any tenderness and compassion, then make my joy complete by being like-minded, having the same love, being one in spirit and of one mind. Do nothing out of selfish ambition or vain conceit. Rather, in humility value others above yourselves, not looking to your own interests but each of you to the interests of the others" (Phil. 2:1–4).

Ask the Lord to help strengthen the trumpet call to intensive prayer, so that it is heard throughout the Church in the U.S.

"Therefore I want the men everywhere to pray, lifting up holy hands without anger or disputing" (1 Tim. 2:8). "Pray continually" (1 Thess. 5:17).

Ask the Lord for the Church to rise up with a strong prophetic voice for America.

"Pray also for me, that whenever I speak, words may be given me so that I will fearlessly make known the mystery of the gospel" (Eph. 6:19).

Pray for a spirit of repentance to fall upon the Church in America that would cause believers to turn back to God and seek Him.

"God looks down from heaven on all mankind to see if there are any who understand, any who seek God" (Ps. 53:2).

Pray for a spirit of courage to rise within the Church, a commitment to endure whatever it takes to see the fulfillment of God's purposes in our nation.

"Be on your guard; stand firm in the faith; be courageous; be strong" (1 Cor. 16:13). "You became imitators of us and of the Lord, for you welcomed the message in the midst of severe suffering with the joy given by the Holy Spirit" (1 Thess. 1:6).

Pray that the Church in America will so noticeably live in Christ's peace that His peace comes into the councils of our nation.

"Let the peace of Christ rule in your hearts, since as members of one body you were called to peace. And be thankful" (Col. 3:15).

Pray for a movement of the Spirit that creates a dramatic cultural transformation in the United States, bringing about a nation that has learned to put its hope in the Word of God.

"Do not conform to the pattern of this world, but be transformed by the renewing of your mind. Then you will be able to test and approve what God's will is—his good, pleasing and perfect will" (Rom. 12:2).

Ask the Lord to awaken the Church to the temporary nature of the nations and to the eternal nature of the reign of God.

"But the wicked will perish: Though the LORD's enemies are like the flowers of the field, they will be consumed, they will go up in smoke" (Ps. 37:20). "But seek first his kingdom and his righteousness, and all these things will be given to you as well" (Matt. 6:33).

Pray that courage born of wisdom will be given to Christians in places of leadership in government, the courts, and law schools across the nation so that they will stand for a godly basis for law.

"Have I not commanded you? Be strong and courageous. Do not be afraid; do not be discouraged, for the LORD your God will be with you wherever you go" (Josh. 1:9). "Then I will teach transgressors your ways, so that sinners will turn back to you" (Ps. 51:13).

Scriptures and Personal Notes to Pray for the Church

5. MEDIA

Pray for truth to be an established standard in our news media.

"In your majesty ride forth victoriously in the cause of truth, humility and justice; let your right hand achieve awesome deeds" (Ps. 45:4).

Pray that media bias will be replaced by fairness.

"The King is mighty, he loves justice—you have established equity; in Jacob you have done what is just and right" (Ps. 99:4). "Do you rulers indeed speak justly? Do you judge people with equity?" (Ps. 58:1).

Ask that Christianity will receive fair coverage in all reports.

"Have I not written thirty sayings for you, sayings of counsel and knowledge, teaching you to be honest and to speak the truth, so that you bring back truthful reports to those you serve?" (Prov. 22:20–21).

Scriptures and Personal Notes to Pray for the Media

6. SPIRITUAL WARFARE

★ ★ ★ ★ ★

Ask for great awareness and discernment for the Lord's praying people as they pray over the election.

"When you go into battle in your own land against an enemy who is oppressing you, sound a blast on the trumpets. Then you will be remembered by the LORD your God and rescued from your enemies" (Num. 10:9). "Be very careful, then, how you live—not as unwise but as wise, making the most of every opportunity, because the days are evil. Therefore do not be foolish, but understand what the Lord's will is" (Eph. 5:15–17).

Pray for physical protection for all candidates and their families throughout this campaign season.

"May the LORD answer you when you are in distress; may the name of the God of Jacob protect you" (Ps. 20:1). "Whoever dwells in the shelter of the Most High will rest in the shadow of the Almighty" (Ps. 91:1).

Plead with the Lord for a strong hedge of protection around the nation itself during this time of decision.

"May your unfailing love be with us, LORD, even as we put our hope in you" (Ps. 33:22).

Scriptures and Personal Notes for Spiritual Warfare over the Election

7. REVIVAL AND SPIRITUAL AWAKENING

★ ★ ★ ★ ★

Pray for another Great Awakening to sweep the nation as the Lord's people learn to humble themselves with a contrite spirit, and to tremble at the Word of the Lord.

"'Has not my hand made all these things, and so they came into being?' declares the LORD. 'These are the ones I look on with favor: those who are humble and contrite in spirit, and who tremble at my word'" (Isa. 66:2).

Ask the Lord to bring revival to the Church in America.

"Oh, that you would rend the heavens and come down, that the mountains would tremble before you! As when fire sets twigs ablaze and causes water to boil, come down to make your name known to your enemies and cause the nations to quake before you! For when you did awesome things that we did not expect, you came down, and the mountains trembled before you. Since ancient times no one has heard, no ear has perceived, no eye has seen any God besides you, who acts on behalf of those who wait for him" (Isa. 64:1–4).

Pray for the preachers of America to fearlessly proclaim the Word of God regarding sin and God's love.

"But God demonstrates his own love for us in this: While we were still sinners, Christ died for us" (Rom. 5:8). "In the presence of God and of Christ Jesus, who will judge the living and the dead, and in view of his appearing and his kingdom, I give you this charge: Preach the word; be prepared in season and out of season; correct, rebuke and encourage— with great patience and careful instruction. For the time will come when people will not put up with sound doctrine. Instead, to suit their own desires, they will gather around them a great number of teachers to say what their itching ears want to hear" (2 Tim. 4:1–3).

Scriptures and Personal Notes to Pray for Revival and Spiritual Awakening

FLASHPOINTS FOR PRAYER

These are areas of controversy, disagreement, division—and sometimes outright hostility—in our nation. Some would pick other issues than what I have listed here, but I believe we must pray over at least these eight areas, praying with discernment and strength:

1. the life of the unborn
2. the nature of marriage and family
3. religious freedom
4. the U.S. relationship with Israel
5. the growing threat of terrorism and the fear and mistrust it brings
6. racism and its growing divisiveness
7. immigration
8. the idolatry of tolerance—and the resulting intolerance for those who disagree with prevailing ideas. This issue greatly impacts the other seven flashpoints.

Scriptures and Personal Notes to Pray for Any of These Flash Points

AMEN IS NOT THE END

★ ★ ★ ★ ★

Prayer rarely stops after the amen. When we passionately cry out to God over any issue, we should, with integrity, find ourselves praying, "and Lord, if there is any way You can use me to be an answer to this prayer, here I am." When we pray for an election, it seems that simple honesty will then require us to follow up our prayer with voting.

What about broadening the prayer effort beyond your own prayers? Why not start a short-term prayer gathering in your home for the 30 or 40 days before the election? Invite friends or those with similar passion to join you each week for a very focused prayer meeting that asks God to intervene in our electoral process.

In a country with nearly 350 million people, it is very easy to feel as though one person is incapable of making a difference. That is false on many levels, particularly when we consider the power of prayer.

As we pray—even as one solitary person—we are teaming up with the Creator of the universe to change situations. The only way that positive change is not possible is when Christians refuse to pray!

ELECTION PRAYER JOURNAL

This space is provided for you to jot down Scriptures and notes, perhaps candidates' names, etc., —anything that you might use to guide and focus your prayers for national, state, and local elections.

National Election

President: _____

_____

_____

_____

_____

Senate: _____

_____

_____

_____

_____

House of Representatives: _____

_____

_____

_____

_____

State Election

Referendums: _____

_____

_____

_____

_____

_____

_____

Governor: _____

_____

_____

_____

_____

_____

Lieutenant Governor: _____

_____

_____

_____

_____

_____

Secretary of State: _____

_____

_____

_____

_____

Other Offices: _____

_____

_____

_____

_____

_____

State Senator: _____

_____

_____

_____

_____

State Representative: _____

_____

_____

_____

_____

Judicial Races: _____

_____

_____

_____

_____

_____

Local City and County Election

Referendums: _____

_____

_____

_____

_____

_____

Mayor: _____

_____

_____

_____

_____

_____

City Council: _____

_____

_____

_____

_____

_____

District Attorney: _____

_____

_____

_____

_____

_____

Sherriff: _____

_____

_____

_____

_____

_____

School Board: _____

_____

_____

_____

_____

Other Offices: _____

_____

_____

_____

_____

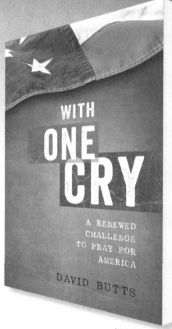

Prayer CONNECT

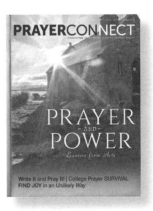  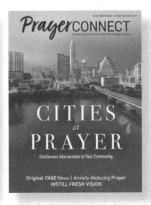

A QUARTERLY MAGAZINE DESIGNED TO:

Mobilize believers to pray God's purposes for their church, city and nation.

Connect intercessors with the growing worldwide prayer movement.

Equip prayer leaders and pastors with tools to disciple their congregations.

Each issue of *Prayer Connect* includes:

- Practical articles to equip and inspire your prayer life.
- Helpful prayer tips and proven ideas.
- News of prayer movements around the world.
- Theme articles exploring important prayer topics.
- Connections to prayer resources available online.

Print subscription: $24.99
(includes digital version)

Digital subscription: $19.99

Church Prayer Leaders Network membership: $35.99 (includes print, digital, and CPLN membership benefits)